Advance Praise

"A *haint* is a term for the dead, but in Teri Cross Davis' hands, *Haint* is a book of life. Not a book of survival, though the poet survives, not a book of reckoning, though the poet comes to terms with many things. *Haint* is a book of choices, and witnessing. A book of learning the bodies, territories, pleasures and sorrows. A book that constructs the irrepressible center of a soul, page by page, plank by plank. A book a reader will put down after reading and mutter *yes* to themselves, haunted."

> — Cornelius Eady, Miller Family Chair, The University of Missouri

"Exploring the psychic interstices of coming-of-age, love, marriage, and motherhood, these meditations on desire, hunger, loss, birth, nurture, and violence raise questions and challenge assumptions about Black woman's selfhood under the sign of *haint*. From the haunting past (ancestors showing in the resoluteness of skin and hair, or speaking from the margins of their eclipsed histories; the memory of parental discord literally marking the body; or, the negotiation of one's sense of belonging, whether in Africa or Ohio) to the unrelenting present with its insistent hungers, the essential terrain here is the primal knowing *(eros)* of girls and women, and the particular valences, both tender and terrible, of such knowing. Teri Cross Davis conveys a grown woman's hard-won wisdom, acknowledging the snares of seeking acceptance or understanding, much less abiding love, in a world where one might be rendered spectral, indecent, or crazy, even. Ultimately, the vulnerabilities, boldness, passion, and fears on display in this moving collection forge a new song of self-affirmation."

> — Sharan Strange, member, Dark Room Collective, and author of *Ash* and the chapbook *The Quotient of Injustice*

"What Teri Ellen Cross Davis writes in her poem *I'll Be There* is an apt description of the power and yearning this book is: 'It's a breaking heart's last hope of reunion....' Although heartbreak is the origin of so many of these poems, it's love that makes them go. Love to which they plead and aspire and pray."

> — Ross Gay, 2016 Kingsley Tufts Prize, 2016 National Book Critics Circle Award, author of *Catalog of Unabashed Gratitude*

"Science tells us that skin is our largest organ. Poet Teri Cross Davis reminds us that skin is both collective history and individual testimony—a maze, a frustration, a celebration. Her extraordinary debut, *Haint*, asks us to consider every consequence of the female form, from the quiet ecstasies of 'Morning Ritual' to the methodical way a woman cuts an apple for her dying father-in-law; pulling no punches, an *Ode to Now 'n' Laters* is chased with a wrenching consideration of pre-teen pregnancy. Davis is a master of shifting dictions to surprise. In *Odalisque,* we venture the perspective not of the central white nude, but of the black maid forced to stand naked behind her: 'You bleed like I bleed / but we ain't friends.' A few pages later, the sonnet *Knell* invites, 'Haunt this empty space if you will.' This collection, which hums and startles, will echo in the reader for months to come."

> — Sandra Beasley, author of *I Was the Jukebox* and *Count the Waves*

"...A deep intelligence governs this work and a struggle to look squarely at a culture—peoples of many cultures in actuality—intentionally wiped clean of its history ... Teri Cross Davis has the courage to make this complex experience come to life, to address it, to let her readers know what it feels like, and to tell them she will go on, facing and giving life to a new level of understanding that is seldom addressed."

> — Myra Sklarew, author of *Harmless*

Haint

poems

by Teri Ellen Cross Davis

Inaugural Publication in the
Giron/Valdez Series for Unique Voices in Literature

Arlington, Virginia

Published by Gival Press, an imprint of Gival Press, LLC.

For information please write:

Gival Press, LLC

P. O. Box 3812

Arlington, VA 22203

www.givalpress.com

First edition

ISBN: 978-1-940724-04-1

eISBN: 978-1-940724-05-8

Library of Congress Control Number: 2016939865

Cover art © Zaretskaya] Dreamstime.com.

Book Design by Ken Schellenberg.

Grateful acknowledgement is made to the following publications and anthologies in which these poems appeared, sometimes in slightly different forms.

ArLiJo: "Letdown", "Family Bed"

Beltway Quarterly: "Passover," "Complected," "Haint," "Knell," "A Piece of Tail," "Charting," "After The Return of the Prodigal Mother by Dawn Black," "Slip Skin Study: Broken," "Induced"

Bum Rush The Page: A Def Poetry Jam: "Complected"

Cave Canem Anthology IV: "Kiwi"

Cave Canem Anthology VI: "Dear Diary"

Check the Rhyme: An Anthology of Female Poets & Emcees': "Understood "

Delaware Poetry Review: "Fade to Black," "Gaze," "Membrane"

Gargoyle: "Morning When a Dream Lingers"

Gathering Ground: A Reader Celebrating Cave Canem's First Decade: "Haint"

Generations: "Southern Cross"

Growing Up Girl: "An Anthology of Voices from Marginalized Spaces: Dear Diary"

Kinfolks: "Why Persephone Should Be a Black Name"

Tempu Tupu!/walking Naked: "Africana Women's Poetic Self-portrait: the blond on his arm," " The kink in the fantasy"

The Why and Later: "Understood"

Torch: "Scar Tissue, the blond on his arm"

Natural Bridge: "Wrath"

Mi Poesias: "Family Bed"

Poet Lore: "After Earl Came Home"

Poetic Voices without Borders 2: "Nights at Maya's"

PuertodelSol blog: "Handicapped Stall," "The Week's End"

The Sligo Journal (Fall 2014/Spring 2015): "At 5 Weeks," "Redemption," "One Night Stand"

The Sligo Journal (Fall 2015/Spring 2016): "Work Calendar," "Sixteen"

Contents

My deepest gratitude to all my past English teachers from high school to college to graduate school, Ohio University, American University, Cave Canem, Soul Mountain, The Virginia Center for the Creative Arts, The Fine Arts Center at Provincetown, and The Folger Shakespeare Library. Special thanks to Kim Roberts, Dan Vera, Michael Gushue, Abby Beckel, Brandon D. Johnson, Mignonette Dooley Johnson, Myra Sklarew, Sharan Strange, Cornelius Eady, Sandra Beasley, Martha Collins, Ross Gay, Judith Harris, Yael Flusberg, Fred Joiner, Alan King, Sarah Browning, Melissa Tuckey, Derrick Weston Brown, Reginald Dwayne Betts, Katy Ritchie, Phillis Levin and all the poets who have encouraged me in the journey to completing this book.

To my family: Burnetta, Raymond, Jack and Vergie, Katie Mae, Eddie Lovelace, Marshall, Tracy, Toni and Tyler, thank you.

To Hayes, Zoe, August and Id: Thank you for inspiring me and giving me time to write.

I dedicate the collection to my husband and first reader, Hayes E.D. Davis,

I could not have done this without you. April, August, Always.

I.

Haint — Southern colloquialism, definition for:
ghost or apparition;
loose woman, a hussy;
lost soul;
scary bitch, mean person, usually a woman

Fade to Black

Only now can pixels completely capture
the mulatto ancestors born in Virginia,
the freedmen of Georgia, the sharecroppers
in Lafayette County, Arkansas, the winters
yellowing successive generations in Cleveland.
Only now does the camera rhapsodize
over the freckles, pale blossoms
continuing their spread, like seeds,
every year, each crop more noticeable
than the last. The lens focuses
on the pores' gentle sag as the skin
ushers in the fourth decade; the areola's
circular spill, nursing's bulls-eye;
the faded ripples, broadening streaks
on the abdomen and thighs, smooth
reminders from their stretching boast
twice taut, now slack; the adolescent scars
on the left inside wrist-the only physical
reminder of a parents' divorce; the darker
brown and black moles— little peppered
volcanoes once seen on Big Ma's face—
now popping up, more each year. A closer
angle spotlights the spiral curl of the hair,
a decade free of chemicals, softer now,
assertive, tangled in reflection. Finally,
the close-up— a mirror, and I am discovering
how slow love is, even slower acceptance,
but traveling down the road I was born to know.

Why Persephone Should Be a Black Name

Crazed with loneliness, edgy
sharp like pale skin, Hades breaks the earth apart
for want of his own piece of sun. The mother,

Demeter is all raging heartbreak. Bares her canine teeth,
grieving bosom to anyone with eyes, to everyone's eyes.

Persephone in a strange land, strange man, stranger hands
finds her chaste determination wrestling a new hunger
until the girl is overcome and finds solace sucking the earthy pulp
of six pomegranate seeds. A mother's streaked pleas

finally clears the path home for her only child. Persephone rises
walks this path of dried tears, meets her mother, a changed woman.

But even a mother's embrace has a time limit. Six months
for her six seeds of solace. For this she must return to the man
whose eyes welled with a need she could never fill.

Translation
But I'm sayin though . . . some crazed dude
rises from no where and grabs Persephone
right outta her momma's arms. Now her moms,

Demeter, is pissed off mo than a bit but ain't nobody
got time for her sob stories, right? So she got to negotiate
(ain't dat some shit) with her daughter's kidnapper.

Persephone, dis po child, she holdin out as long as she can
hungrier than a motherfucka and finally, she eats 6
of these seeds. Meanwhile her moms is working a deal,

(not sure if money changed hands) and fixes it
so that Persephone can come back home,
but those six seeds hauntin her ass.

And it turns out, just for those damn seeds
she got to stay for half duh damn year
in some place she never asked to be.

East 149th Street (Symphony for a Black Girl)

sitting too long
skinny cinnamon burnt legs
cramped, Momma's thigh
suctioned your ear
relief was turning your head
a new view of the television

but nothing was better than
matching candy-colored beads
symmetrical cornrows
braids swinging rhythmically
aluminum sneaking its shine
through the hair's woven layers

and the freedom of skipping
on sidewalks, blacktopped driveways,
running round backyards, listening
to the beads clanging kiss
the crescendo then whispering—this
music celebrating the movement of you

Complected

What the fine rain does not hide and cannot wash away
are coal fingers shrugging slicker strings tighter, protecting
just-straightened hair. The humidity is deadly to this delicate

process, and can nap the nape along the kitchen instantly,
reverting to the natural curl she dreads.The girl beside her
wears no slicker but has a ponytail like Barbie's and is just

as fair. The pubescent boys stare. She's an urban Venus,
waiting for the same bus. The hooded girl is not Venus.
Dark brown is not beauty—darker still a death sentence

if you are young, waiting for a bus, a long appreciative
glance, even catcalls, "hey redbone" love. The hooded
girl hopes the Korean store up the street will have a sale

soon on fading cream and human hair,
because there is always a price for beauty.

My Monthly

Warm, gray and smooth—the back seat
of Granddad's Park Avenue
greeted me like a mug of hot chocolate
on a blistering cold Cleveland day
or a heating pad to a sore, cramping abdomen.

I could imagine my father's voice as he called,
Pop, Teri's got those bad cramps again, can you…
And I wish I could have seen my grandfather's face
because the men never talked of such things in his day.
But my grandfather would wait for me,

parked outside the school doors, a refuge
from uncomfortable chairs, seizing side pains,
stained jeans and bulky school-issued sanitary napkins,
motor running; heat blasting, warming, transforming
the backseat's gray leather into a subtle embrace.

Ode to Now 'n' Laters

Tucked under her pillowcase
heaven is a roller-filled toss away.
The night cut by the sound
of unwrapping candy—silence
before each saturated fold
is peeled away, revealing
apple, banana, pineapple, or sweet, tart cherry.

Always now, now, now, never later
as the moon winks in slick approval
from an otherwise cold adult sky. But here
yields glory exploding on her tongue,
juice filling her mouth
so much so, she smacks her lips,
breaking the night's polite rules.

In this dank cave she calls a mouth,
every taste bud is hollering hallelujah,
called to witness how the essence of a thing
only softens when stretched and sucked so hard
the mouth's roof pays in tender.

And in the mouth's wet joy, all parties
become malleable, teased apart with teeth,
cajoled to reunion by a happy tongue.
Candy shares its secrets now, how
much sugar, corn syrup, artificial flavors
and dyes, until she arrives at its heart,
its ephemeral moment, when a thing is
the most it will ever be and no more.

This is the pulse of the god of pleasure—
seduction and destruction in one last
brutally beautiful swallow. And all the mouth is
wondering is when will it happen again?
So who can blame her? Once awakened
all she does is eat another (now)
and another (now) until she falls back asleep
and satisfaction is the enamel's slow erosion.

Fifteen

Growing up, men
were silk suits, smooth
as satin falsettos, rolling,
gliding, dipping, running
away in sweet imagination.

Then I saw Dionysus in leather pants.
Jim Morrison's nipples, posterized,
stared back at me, *Hello,*
I love you and in response
a stirring I knew not how to chase.

But when Jimi's vulnerable ache
found me, I knew there was room
in his bed as the traffic lights
turned blue, fuel for my want
its blundering beginning.

Dear Diary

5/96
he always be over after everybody go to work
when first period bell would be ringin
if we wuz in school
I like him best outta all the boys
when he asks
I let him put it in me
I figure dat make him my boyfriend now

8/96
it's Friday
Grandma's fryin fish
I dreamt about eatin some
So I just can't get enough
grandma is lookin at me funny
but mom is laughin
callin me her new garbage disposal
but I must be sick or somethin
cuz I keep throwin everythang back up

10/96
I'm getttin fat
jus a little cuz I can't fit
my favorite pair of jeans
my boyfriend be like, *oh, it's all good*
since he like his women thick
me—I'm his woman
I can't wait to see what he got me for my 13th birthday

1/97
mom's trippin

keep askin' me if I'm pregnant
cuz I'm all fat and stuff
dat bitch just jealous
cuz I got a man
and she ain't been able to keep one
since we moved in with Grandma last year

3/97
my stomach is killin me
I think I got gallstones or somethin
I'm scared to say anythin though
but this shit feels like I'm gon die or somethin

3/97
Turns out I *was* pregnant
I got a son now
I'm gonna name him LaShae

6/97
my baby daddy live with us now
he ain't goin to school no more
besides, that teacher that got him arrested was trippin anyway
he slangin so we got fly clothes and everythang
and he can ball
he keep sayin he goin to the NBA
dat would be da shit
I hope it happens

8/97
LaShae was actin funny
crying all night

I told my man to get him
cuz shit I ain't gotta do everythang
he hit me and was like *get the fuck up*
I was like nigguh bunk dat I'm tired
da baby just probably fell off da couch or somethin
he be alright
mommy say I gotta let him cry
that I be spoilin him anyway
holdin him all the time
whatevah

11/97
mom ain't goin watch da baby tonight
damn, she be trippin
and Grandma at church
so I gotta take him wid me

just came back from my girl's
we smoked a philly and chilled out
they all think LaShae is the cutest baby
he had on his Baby Gap outfit
I know I'm lucky to have a man like mine
it sucks sometimes but I'm happy we live together

1/98
9th grade is hard
LaShae don't cry as much at night
so at least I can sleep

3/98
yesterday I picked up LaShae

his chest felt all soft and squishy
my cousin called 911
ain't nobody know what happened to him
why he wuz like dat
they just said he probably fell off da couch or somethin

by the time we got to da hospital
my son was dead
he was only 11 months old
now he gone

4/98
the police arrested LaShae's daddy today
told me he killed the baby
that he beat him up and killed him
my brother said if they put him in jail
he can get one of his boys to shank him

what am I gonna tell everybody at school?

I'll Be There

I.
It's Friday night, I'm
at Howard University
talkin' shit to your mother
over the dorm phone.
The Jackson 5 are on
the radio, so I tell her,
just like the song, baby
call my name and. . .
So she says it. Saturday
I'm in Cleveland knocking
on your grandmother's
door. Your mother answers
her big belly poking out
all round and brown.
The Jackson 5 cartoon
is on and so is that song.

II.
Thirty five years later
I am grateful for the phone's
distance, masking my face
as my father relays
his tale. His voice is worn
down to wonder. The acid
of divorce forgotten.
He has found a pitch
even MJ couldn't reach.
It's a breaking heart's
last hope of reunion
dusted off, playing

in the background. How
the needle glides down
into the groove before
the scratches appear,
before the warping,
before the breaking.

Scar Tissue

"Baby just put yo pinkie finger in my drink
cuz it needs some mo sugah." Dad's friend Ronald
is all love with a pistol and a Jheri curl. Mom's friend Tammy
dates rock stars, lives in skintight jeans and a black Camaro.
My parents love to party with their Luther Vandross
and frozen grapes for ice cubes and we gobble it all:
the attention, the laughter, the dank smell of fun
blowing past our upturned faces.

I know I'll never love this way again
I know I'll never love this way again

The arguments begin like my period
early—unpredictable—bloody.
Dressing for school, blasting Prince, his
guitar riffs muffling the cursing, the punches.
Breaking up their fights becomes ritual
like bad cramps, like staining favorite outfits.

I know I'll never love this way again
I know I'll never love this way again

When my daddy moves out, the Wild Irish Rose,
cough syrup and Kool-Aid mixture isn't enough.
So it's swallowing seven or eight aspirin
but I failed Chem. So I try scissors, straight razors,
a messy maze of tender scars and long-sleeve t-shirts.
I try to do this right—cut deep enough
bleed long enough—hoping I'm enough
to bring them back together.

I know I'll never love this way again
I know I'll never love this way again

Akron at Night

A few months after dad left,
the divorce still pending, my mother
drives home on an unspectacular
Cleveland night, looks at me

and says, *Let's drive to Akron.* We're
cuddled in her tiny black Chevy Spectrum,
a stick she taught herself to drive
because it was the cheapest on the lot.

Prince's Batman soundtrack plays
in the cassette player. *Akron.*
Neither of us had ever been there.
It was just the place you drove past to get

home. Prince croons *Vicki Waiting.*
We sing along to the opening night, probing
the wound of the road, hugging tight to highway 77.
When we reach Akron, its lit spires bathe us

in a strange orange glow. The bricked sidewalks
spill out in quiet perfection. Our satisfaction
surrounds us, hanging thick in the closeness of the car.
The cassette clicks, flips, and side B begins.

Free

My mother tells me quickly not rushed but in one breath.
Your brother's wheelchair rolled down the driveway. He fell.
His choice of curse words for this circumstance was a very quiet
oh shit. With force, she measures the details, telling me of the stitches
first, then *they gave him Fentanol, he's not eating*—she's in familiar
territory now—*he tells me, mommy it hurts, I'm keeping him out of school
for a few days*. Our conversation turns to standard fare; financial advice,
lamentations about weight. The quiver having passed through us for now,
even the phone line's static has subsided. The boy will be fine in time.
And the image loops in my head. I see the curved black tongue of the driveway,
its mouth opening to the residential street; its eagerness to spill my brother
into some red Taurus' unsuspecting bumper. I can imagine fear that makes
a raucous thirteen year-old boy whisper *oh shit, oh shit, oh shit*. I can see
how his rough hands must have fumbled for the brakes. And the image loops
in my head. I can see my brother held captive by the safety belts. I can see
the chair hurtling down the driveway's bumpy hill, as if it wanted to see how
the neighbor's grass grows, where wheelchairs cannot travel, as if it wanted
my brother to see what it felt like to be free.

Mercy

One rarely has good memories of a hospital:
no first loves; no fat, healthy summer days;
no pink scraps of dawn; instead, like a hangnail,

the mind catches on the soft hush of disposable
hospital shoe covers, the metallic rungs sweeping
privacy curtains closed, the shadows of shoulders

slumped, shuddering in grief. My mom taught me
to play gin rummy in a hospital. It was the day
the doctors stopped my baby brother's heart,

sewed it up, started it again. We stole the blanket
they returned him in, as if we needed a fabric reminder
of the seconds his heart was still, of the hours we waited,

playing rummy to 1,000 and 1,000 and 1,000 again.
Years later, it's that smell I can't forget: crisp, medicinal,
even after countless cleanings, the retained scent of sweat,

tainted with fear. Thin white blankets, freshly folded
on the foot of my boyfriend's father's bed. And when
I cannot look at his family huddled in shock and sorrow,

adjusting to the verdict of cancer, I look at the blankets,
the hospital name stamped in blue, on every single blanket.
Mercy. Between the memorized route to the cafeteria,

dry erase boards for the next nurse to mark her name,
the yellow sad faces to measure pain, how is this compassion,
a leniency from God? Show me the grace in tearing holes

in the hearts of six month-old babies? The charity of cancer, eating families away, father by grandfather? Erase the stink of hospital from my nostrils, let my grief be dirty and jagged. I have no need for mercy.

The Handicapped Stall

When most 13 year-olds don't want to be seen with their parents,
my mother is pushing my brother into the women's bathroom.
For a moment I don't recognize her. It's only the familiarity of her

motions that brings it all back. Because she still has to bathe
my brother, change his diapers, we are here, in the second floor
bathroom at Cleveland Clinic. As we await yet another surgery

for Tyler, I ask if she wants help. I follow her
to the biggest stall— the handicapped stall. Here she lifts
my 114-pound brother out of his wheelchair and lays him

on the bathroom floor. I had never considered the world
from this angle. She lifts his hips, yanks down his size 14
husky boy cords to reveal the ripe outcome of the earlier

suppository. My brother yells *No!* Inside this stall his anguish,
determined and adamant, reverberates off wet tiles and spotted
sinks and pierces my chest. My hands shake then stop.

Fourteen years ago while doing my hair my mother told me
she was pregnant. She wondered about keeping the child,
not my father's, if she, a single divorcee was ready

for the whole thing again. Now I look at my mother's back
wondering , who is this woman that I failed to recognize? Who,
unguarded, unashamed, moves with a sureness and acceptance

of what must be done. With his limited vocabulary, is it my
presence my brother is rejecting? What 13 year-old wants his
big sister to change his shitty diaper, if not this, what can he hold

private? I take what she hands me, open the stall door carefully,
quickly—try not to afford any unsuspecting eyes a glimpse of this
circumstance. It does not matter the bathroom is empty, except

for my brother's eyes, his head turned to the side, seeing
but unseeing the other stalls, the back ends of toilets,
the uniform cold and gray linoleum, the porcelain pipes running.

Sixteen

I was green.
A tendril reaching
for the weak sun
of early spring.
I wanted laughter,
a male's gaze
to frame a love
worth believing,
but I was wet
still forming.
So the bustle
continued, faces
passing. I thought
my want a curing
a purity that would
redeem me. I was foolish
in this and all things.

Brown Sugar

I.
Once I found
a small crystal
on my inner thigh
brown, angular
I put it to my lips
it was sweet.

II.
Seventeen years-old,
cut-off shorts, sunlight
streaming through a backseat
window spotlighting
skinny, freckled thighs-
tight, supple and soft.
Is this what the fuss is about?

III.
Birthmark #2
patch like a bruise.
Rounded sun
flared edges
thumbprint in brown ink.
I see you. I see you
left thigh.

IV.
At sixteen, my page school
dorm room, alone with my crush.
I press play on the pink
cassette player. Bryan Ferry's

Slave to Love fills the room.
We dance, fingers laced tightly.
An Irish boy French-kissing
a Black girl. I'm lost
in the sensation of his tongue
swimming in my mouth. How
the muscle's slippery warmth,
sweet insistence calls
and the thighs quiver
in response. My knees sway
in praise, as my body thrums;
our tongues tuning,
discovering a deeper rhythm.

V.
Minutes later he would leave me,
afraid either of being caught on the girls floor
or being caught kissing a black girl.
I was never sure which was worse.

II.

Understood

Black women are not supposed to turn
Black men in for rape. Never seen the rule
but I know it's written down somewhere
maybe, underneath the threadbare sheets of my twin bed,
or on the stucco wall he threw me against.
Maybe it's behind the three weeks afterward
when I never left my apartment. Maybe he
just shook it out of me and it crawled into some gutter
and hid out with all my *no's, stop, please.* Can't recall
where I've seen it or how I heard about it but I know it's there
like a scar I carry inside somewhere I can't see, somewhere
that still makes me cry sometimes, especially when I hear
he still breathes, walks, and even wonders on occasion how I am.

Membrane

the hymen wants to
please me cure me glorify me
make an entrance upon breaking

where *shame guilt relief* stain
cold water and soap knuckle out
please come out   don't let her see   don't let him see

farmer   if your crops spot
if drought digs in
the ground refuses to flourish

grab your daughters   if they be virgins
drown them in the nearest lake
brick them into a nearby well

block them from the peeking sun   brick
by blood by brick   do it carefully
so the gods see   and reap your returns

Wrath

For Yvette Cady and other women who have felt it

First I feel the wetness, sudden,
spreading like shame saturating
my blouse, my skirt, my slip.
The smell of gasoline washes
over me like an overpowering cologne.
I realize the origin, the Sprite bottle
in my estranged husband's hand.
I think, Roger I will get to you
in just a moment, I have a customer waiting.
Then I hear the whir and click
of the lighter and heat leans into
me for a kiss. Flame eats the air
from his hand to my skirt, my blouse,
my bra, flame consuming its way to my
face like a hungry lover's mouth.
A new smell, at once familiar,
unnerving: burning hair.
Heat's breath is in my face.
My face is melting, dripping
into my hands. Now, as flames
lick my ears, Roger opens his mouth:
Bitch, how pretty are you now?

Passover

teenage suicide
female bomber
delivering death
camouflaged vagina
cervix sewn
holding 6 pounds
of dynamite tight

Searching

I ask the cabdriver,
Where in Africa
are you from?
Unasema kiswahili?
my American tongue
is dumb, cannot explain
I'm not the average homeboy.

The servants' quarters where I lived
had no washing machines, so every Sunday
with brush and bucket, I scrubbed my old Levi's,
on my knees, back aching, hands rubbed raw.
So much red dirt, my jeans could never be clean enough.
They told me the guard would do my laundry
if I paid him American dollars. It would
make him happy they said. I scrubbed harder.

Are you slimming? White girls
back home die to be this thin.
Here in Kenya I am an oxymoron
black and American.

My people have kept some things:
like this groomed fertile swell
half a basketball attached
to the ironing board of my back.
At some bar in East Nairobi, a man
grabbed two handfuls of my ass,
ran back to his friends, two thumbs up.

Are you Luo? What a mental fuck.

I am the bastard of Uncle Sam
and Mother Africa is senile,
does not recognize her child's child.
Who to claim this society of mutts?
You are low to the ground like the Luo.
I tell them my grandmother is tall
like the Masai.

Rain makes red rivers of their homes,
the ants are building again.
Up go these impossible towers
from cracks in the pavement that lead to my door.
When high enough, I will kick them down,
relishing my small power. I want them
to build their doomed homes again,
smug, anticipating their destruction.
Stupid African ants, don't they
know when they are broken?

This sprawling white palace
was once a colonial home.
Now it's Kileleshwa, a rich
Kenyan suburb. My room
was the servants quarters,
a courtyard, clothesline
stone kitchen. I came here
the newest renovation
African-American.
I left, black American.

Nights at Maya's

As always, I arrive with the Scottish mzungu
eventually his presence will stop getting us
faster service. He starts by ordering Tusker and we
are armed with conversation on observations.

Once in their eyes I was probably a prostitute.
What black woman hangs with white men?
So I told them, *Mimi ni wanafunzi*
I am a student, so don't give me those tsk tsk's.

When I place my order- *nyama choma* with goat,
I know I saved a chicken's life when he comes
running out from the pen in the back of the restaurant
to thank me. The servers don't know why I laugh.

Because it is tradition, I wash my hands
in the dirty bowl the little boy carries from table to table,
before cupping the steaming *ugali* and *nyoma choma*
to my lips like prayer. This is what I will remember

from Kenya. Not the woman around the corner
selling ripe mangoes, brown eggs with feathers,
fresh food my stomach will not process. Not the planned
monthly riots with crimson-tainted rifle butts, the two-handed

gropes in gaudy bars but the long nights at Maya's
a belly full of roasted goat stewed in onions, tomatoes,
maybe *irio* or chips, and maize porridge for capturing the juices,
spinning theory under a spread and studded sky.

Southern Cross

From within the guarded colonial gates
of our Kileleshwa living quarters, Malcolm,
the Scottish intern, and I spice our secured

boredom by overturning courtyard benches,
piling and scaling them like vines to the roof.
Tilting our heads, we soak up the velvet night,

awash in silence so darkly foreign and complete
with its glimmering configurations only seen south
of the equator. Growing up in Little Rock, my momma

told me of her night sky, of following stars' paths with one
brown finger. Growing up in Cleveland, the city's northern
lights drowned out the Big Dipper, Cassiopeia, Orion's belt,

but across the world in Kenya, I can see the Milky Way,
the Southern Cross and I am ensorcelled by the night's
dictation, such incandescent writing on the blackest of sheets.

Piece

From the apartment's balcony
my girlfriends and I could see
their pale skins, hear the clipped
accents. The soldiers were British
and drunk. With money flowing
the Kenyan women became
willing, every stare, every gesture
intoxicating. They tore shirts, teased
skirts, revealed panties, gyrating,
taunting those English boys who'd
never seen such chocolate breasts,
with nipples painted ebony and
Hips rounded to such a swelling
you needed two hands for the grabbing
but oh, they'd heard how wild
black cats can be—scratching backs,
lusty animals in vaguely human skins.
Watching the soldiers took me back
to Ohio University's Frat Row. Those
flushed-faced men, with their backwards
baseball caps, alcohol-emboldened, leering;
the slur in their voices calling me out.
Even then, I was afraid of being that exotic,
kin to these Kenyan women. When are we not
dancing brown bodies, somewhere, swaying
for dollars or pounds, moving at whatever price
black women are selling for these days?

Perspective

The stench erases all
furiously climbing
in your nostrils
out your mouth
obliterating sweet words
about this Kenyan park.

The guide warned you to stay
in the vehicle but the Scottish intern
who hopped out now beckons you
and together you approach the lip
of the alkaline lake, its elemental
foam dirty, tainted in your American eye.
Your brown hand contrasts the black
volcanic ash. You spy a spark of white—
brushing it off, you see it clearly now,
a feather, and as you tilt your chin
to the charcoal-edged horizon
there's a fluttering pink dash
flitting like the wind-possessed hem
of a slip, huddling en masse,
thousands of wild flamingos.

The rented blue NGO van fades,
the Ethiopian scholar and Kenyan staff
too sensible or too jaded to venture
into this vaguely protected wilderness
fade. And it's just you and the Scot
who see this sight. And it's just you
who sees this sight and this tarred
white feather is all you have
to remember it by.

The kink in the fantasy

After the sex, the condensation of bent
limbs spent, unfolding to the slowing
rag of exhausted breathing, she knows
she can't sleep here. Not with kinked hair

sweated out, matted and limp like overcooked
fettucine. If she were alone, she would
take the time, part it, grease it, let the fingers
dance their nightly routine of sliding across

scalp, sectioning hair, pirouetting twists.
And after the cursive braiding, donning
the green and black silk scarf, tying
the knot her fingers can do in their sleep.

But if she unveiled this ritual before his
sleepy blue eyes who would he see? *Aunt Jemima?*
Mammy? Not Bottecilli's *Venus* or a Raphael's *Madonna*
but broken black hair strands, oil stains on his cotton

pillowcase. So she mutters something about
an early meeting, breaks the embrace. Smiling,
apologizing, smiling, apologizing, she locates
tossed clothing. She gets dressed. She goes home.

One Night Stand

If this is desire, let *consumption's*
pace leave the body *spiritless.*
Let the next morning's tears be *expectoration;*

ejecting the ether of guilt, *an*
absolution of action, flesh *indignant*
of limits imaginary, arbitrary. Hear the *robin's*

glory sear the day, *resolute*—
the deed is done, lust was your *donation.*

Morning When a Dream Lingers

Paint the sky slate gray. Streak
cornflower blue with rain. Layer
wisps of a singer's voice yearning,

aching and familiar. Make this
a scene, stolen and framed from
some forgettable film, its protagonist

beautiful, unobserved and broken.
Give her kinky hair, make her brown
and this will be a film you've never

seen. Here, touch is not a physical
sensation but analytical, wistful,
hollow like a word, like a vestige.

Ask yourself how long do you wait
to get out of bed? When do you rein
in the ghosts, silence them, get up, live?

Kiwi

hairy brown belies fresh morning hue inside
bare walls, decorate warm—new love

anticipation, tenderly rolling the kiwi, a supple palm
continue worship of him, days indiscriminate

kiwi soft, pliable, temptation sin
loving this much, so soon, so full

ripe subtle puncture, peeling slowly, green discovered
days, we'll be new again, relearn

juice running the length of the thumb, extend tongue
like animals marking every room, a musky scent

teeth sink in flesh, wet lips kiss upon contact
glutted, soon we will expand beyond this place

Church

ten forty-five on Sunday morning
is the church of a naked body
   pressed   the sermon of
his penis inside
me not wet—opening
palms slowly
praying on his hipbones
steadying myself
because there is still   time

Process

Kitchen

Mommy would warm press my hair
if I begged and pleaded. When I got older,
I bought an electric hot comb and thought I was free,
locking myself in the bathroom so my white roommates
wouldn't smell my burning hair.

She got Indian in her

My fingers glide through
my aunt's wavy black ink;
it spills, loving her shoulders:
Deb, you got such good hair.
She slaps my hand hard, demanding,
What does that mean?

Afro picks

My father's was bleached wood, could pull apart
leaving a sheath with tiny holes, a home for the straightened
metal wires. It was a stamp of pride, like the African figurine
bookends with their tight carved coils, supporting my parents'
favorite books: Giovanni, Angelou, Castañeda.

Jigaboo

The back of the bus was reserved,
like the boys' affections,
for light-skinned girls with straight or wavy hair.
Dark-skinned and nappy girls need not apply.

Mixed

I marvel over my husband's hair—
the lapping curl is his black father's,
the fineness is his white mom's.
His hair tells his story, if it can't be read from his skin.

Aunt Jemima blues

What black woman doesn't hate to lay a freshly greased head
on a cotton pillowcase?
What black woman doesn't hesitate to explain her hairscarf
to his white relatives?
What black woman doesn't hate defining the particulars of herself?

Soul Sister fro

When the beautician cut out my relaxer, I wasn't afraid
of who greeted me in the mirror: I see a snapshot of my mother
a 1967 teenager in Little Rock; in the next one, she's a new mother,
a dusky angel in a bikini with a charcoal halo, honeymooning in
      Miami, 1973.

Crowned

Sometimes I wrap my hair. The fabric
gives me a silhouette, a bun
fastened tightly in the back,
tempted my fingers want to spring
what's bound underneath:
the kinked curls and the complicated naps.

You tenderheaded?

I am teaching my husband
how the first tooth of a comb
defines the line, how to grease
the exposed scalp, how to massage
thru the kink in each curl.

I am relearning how to cornrow:
knuckles kneading the tender,
separating the rough.

Like I did, he has to learn
to love the plait,
to love the part.

After Earl Came Home

He lies on the eve his death calling out to me,
the only woman in the house, his new
daughter-in-law. He gestures toward a ripe
fruit basket, a gift of solace to his sons.
My hand wavers, anxious to please, unsure
if the duty is right. I select the reddest of apples,
cupping its firm body into my palm. Silently
I slip to the kitchen, wash away pesticides, polish,
to peel the fruit. Red wrapping curls reveal the white
interior. Now the real work begins as I core
the apple, steadying my hand to slice
the crescents, smoothly, clean curves a dying
artist can appreciate. I sneak back to his side,
careful to avoid my brother-in-law, a licensed
nurse sure to disapprove. Complicit, I slide
the nude pieces to his trembling hands, thinking
this secret I can keep—how grateful he is
for this last taste of Eden.

Work Calendar

As easy as I swipe the dry eraser
the board is clean, white—gone is the day
your dad died. February spills in, fills
candy hearts with sayings replacing
the Christmas card you will never send him,
the presents you will never give or receive again.

You approach this Christmas slow. The roads to you,
once familiar to me, I travel on slowly now,
your grief a black ice. How I wish for snow

to bury your hurt clean
and take the bite out of the air.

Lily

I. On Stage

When you dance
I see the disconnect
between the hips undulations,
the pole grinds and the deadened
eyes. I have hidden too,
known the tenderness
masked by exposed flesh,
thoughtless easy breast,
tight outlines of the v of sex.
I know showing it all, once done,
is nothing. After the dance,

you work the tables,
stopping at each one,
chatting up customers
for crumpled bills.
I hand you mine,
not for the cheap red wine,
sticky wet tabletop,
bright flashing lights,
your ploy of a dance.
I hand you crumpled bills,
because I want you
to forgive me for taking
the easy way out.

II. Back Stage

Thighs taut, I balance myself

inches above the toilet seat, touch
the door handle with tissue.
Pull the napkin to dry my hands
before I wash them. Then I see you.
You run in. I hear the liquid
rush from your body to the bowl.
You emerge, search for my eye.
I dry my hands. Our conversation
begins gently, like a kiss between
first-time lovers. I compliment your
teddy bear backpack while around us
women routinely adjust sequined thongs,
glittering push-up bras. You tell me
of your young son, his teddy bear backpack
you wear as talisman. Impulsively
I grab your hands, hold them warmly.
It is a beautiful bag. I just wanted you
to know.

III. Front Door

Upon entry to the club,
we promised the bouncer
to treat his girls right.
We drank the two drink
minimum. Tipped when
prompted. Then Lily stepped
from the stage. Sat with us,
talked of her Connecticut
upbringing, wealthy family,
big lawn, white picket-fences.

Said she missed her father.
We whispered to each other,
Yeah right, whose story was that?
Some memorized T.V. movie of the week.

Walking out, we told the bouncer,
we had a good time. Then Lily
slinked past him, broke the door's
threshold burst into a warm New Orleans
night and was real—
blonde hair darkly wet,
skin pink and flushed.
I wanted to tell you good-bye
she said, eyes sparkling. She was
breathless. This was her story to tell.

the blond on his arm

wonder if she works out all day
if *he* pays for her trainer
if she even has a job
then she is blond which is a different
category than white   blond has its own
story   its own golden fabric and myth
add blond to white and automatically
he is out of my league always
no matter how much I scrub
in the morning showers
the dark patches on elbows
and knees won't go away
only red replaces them
raw after disgust has its turn
black is my soul they say
black is my skin they say
brown is my skin I say
and the only color
my soul knows
is longing

Odalisque

After Untitled (Boudoir scene of nude white woman and her naked
        black maid, 1850's) by Félix-Jacques Moulin.

He ask her *up on this couch, please.*
Leopard skin under her bottom
like she know something of it.
Tell me, *take off your dress, sit here.*
See these breasts, how they hang?
Used, by they babies not mine;
these shoulders, sagging so low.
I work all damn day, now this.
She done snuck her leg under mine,
snake. You bleed like I bleed
but we ain't friends. We ain't sisters.
You smile for his camera. I'm here
'cus it's my job. You take this picture,
make me sit behind you. Prop like that
leopard skin. And you sit, coy-like,
pretty-like. We ain't sisters, we ain't
friends. Just tell me when I can get up
put my dress back on, be done
with your foolishness. White woman,
smile now, they all want you
until they don't.

Gaze

Because I want to be seen
I strip down   off comes
Josephine's feather skirt
Sarah's prodigious bottom
Dorothy's come-hither stare
Aunt Jemima's red kerchief
Mammy's wide bosom
National Geographic's tribal nakedness
History in each garment on the floor

Not full frontal, nor profile
Not the background
Nor the body reclining
Standing, I name myself
Shedding the fiction of availability
Becoming nonfiction
Let the prose of me
Gild your tongue
Separate the double-speak
Fingertip, lip to limb
You read the tome of my skin
This body in a new language—my own

She Talks to Michael Fassbender

Sorceress of ebony thighs, Child of midnights./I prefer to all things,
      opium and the night
from Charles Baudelaire's "La Vénus Noire"

Don't be so simple. This can work.
But I need you to get real here.
Brown girls don't get fairy tales.
The world has an edge; I know

I can fall off. Just being pretty
don't cut it for me. No one is throwing
a cloak over a puddle. Even my fairy
godmother got laid off in the recession.

My ideal man needs strength, not just
muscle. He needs equal parts charisma
and intensity, bravado and hustle.
Throw in a dash of game. From

Fishtank to *Macbeth,* swagger translates
well on your slim Irish hips. Leashed
carnality in the low gravel of your
voice, a blue-eyed stare, a chin so chiseled

it makes a woman wanna holler *Hot damn!*
Michael, please, brown girls don't get
to be damsels, we don't get the rom-com
(except as the sassy friend) or period pieces

with corsets, proper lust on slow burn. Hold up!
You proposing to be the white knight, fully-equipped

with a castle and happily ever after? Do I get
the pedestal? Well, admittedly I'm down

for being swept up. Will you hold the broom though?
I have to work in the morning. C'mon Michael,
Spades is still trump so show me what you working
with baby. I got the deuce, you got the ace?

The small of my back (your hand here)

ripples inside a sculpted valley
smooth frets step stone
stroke down slowly
find the indent
junction of
before/after
the pause in
flesh's swing
delicious dip for
tongue thumb or
palm the pelvic flair
contours induce cupping
how subtle slides to saturated
curves this sacred stop can steer
or induce, glisten then arch. Follow or lead.

Permission

This folded world unfurls
as your lips brush the petals.
Before you my apex
extends its wet invitation.
Soon you will want
release, a stream of stars—
but first contemplate
how beauty layers itself,
want slick in this vestibule.

He Can Get The Panties

Be they silk, cotton,
nylon mix, thong,
boycut, bikini, but
not the grannies.
Leg by leg we step in,
cover the triangle,
be it landing strip, bush,
or bald. Hoisted up,
bunched in hand, fingers
around the rim, flipping
elasticized edges smooth.
We say *he can get the panties*,
because the flimsy fabric
is all that shields the world
from gaping want, dewy musk
our *cassolette*—we say *panties*,
because this is the language
we have for desire, even then,
ladies, well, don't discuss *want*.
We giggle, coquettishly lower eyes,
cross legs, press together thighs—demure.
While the panties contain our hidden cliffs,
and under the mons pubis,
pink hoods tremble awake but
are still held back in print or lace.
We say *the panties*, and even then
it's a *little* dirty, underwear, too formal
drawls too street, the vernacular
filthy on the tongue. Because
this all must be neat, like
panties with bows on them.

Women aren't supposed to
desire openly, talk about honeyed lust
trickling inside our thighs, the heat
that arises, wets those panties,
because he, *he can get the panties*
move them to the side, stick them
under a pillow, drop them in haste
on the floor, *he can get the panties*
as long as we can arch our backs,
grind our hips, bite his shoulder
make him call our name, over and over again.

The Dark Lady Speaks

"And Sylvia—witness heaven that made her fair— / Shows Julia but
    a swarthy Ethiope."
(II. vi. 25-26) *The Two Gentlemen of Verona*

Bet you love these wires on my head. These
breasts of dun, lips full for fun, my mound so
round, cheeks softest cushions for pushing. I'm no
angel air, smoke's on my breath. White boy, please

see my dark rhythm and gyrating hips?
The devil whispers to my black cat. I
thought you liked it like that? Scratching your back?
Thirsty for my exotic? Gulp, don't sip.

My sauce you suck from your fingerstips.
My candy beckons you, sour and sweet.
But it's Blonde Becky, you wifey. My black

ass, always cast in shadow plays. Don't trip
let's be real, in or out the sheets, I'm still
the one you screw, then say, fuck that, fuck black.

III.

Haint

no amount of dilation and suction
hemorrhaging and fever
could have erased you or
the pulp of your carved initials
made with the solid grasp
of a still forming hand

science tells me
inside my bones
you are still whispering
that years from now
cut me to the marrow
and microscopes will read
the rings of your insistent story
no matter the inconvenient
coupling of timing and desire

even now when the bloody show
disappoints our sharpening hunger
do you still cling or are you willing
to let another call my womb
home?

Charting

cycle 3
My thighs have a new language:
softness. Stirring a new sound is
need. Not the moist sap of him
leaving me, need him back but
a purposeful need and it grows
in every touch, waiting.

cycle 7
Pencils, thermometer, finger measuring
my sap (does it stretch more than three inches,
is it crumbly and white?) My grandmother says,
I didn't know you could plan these things.

Without plans what are we?
Elderly fathers, adolescent mothers.
Explain tectonic shifts, thermal currents, sunspots
Without planning, the yawning chaos swallows us
with darkness spawning forever like Arizona sky.

Do we not plan when we think our god will welcome us in heaven?

cycle 12
The ache rocks itself now
and the potential that lines
the body shudders out
in monthly complaint.
We   are   trying.
What was once expelled
as nuisance, I hold my heels
cradling and hope is as fragile

as this tenuous milky liquid
drying to a flaky film
underneath me.

Knell

The needles lie unused, my hand grips
  the table. I shudder to expel what I long
  to keep—the pain sweetens to cleanse in long
  steady strokes. The nurse tightens her grip.
Soft suctioned skull holds the warm spot,
  size of a fingernail. The pain keeps me still,
  fills the silver pan ringing now silent now still.
  Cramps for your epitaph, gravestone—this bloody spot.
Haunt this empty womb if you will.
  Come again, dancing bringing life and death
  to suffocate this pain and hide its blooms.
  Come again baby and consume me whole, I will
  keep your life, hang mine in chance for death
  to birth you and be life and death blooming.

The First IVF Fails

Speeding down Strandhill's suburban sidewalk
6 houses down to your best friend's house.
You drop the bike, let it clang to the ground
while you run up to ring Jay's backyard doorbell.

You don't think that by letting the bike fall
you could jar a brake loose, break a pedal.
You're 7, you slam hard on the coaster
brakes because a sideways skid looks cool.

You don't think about damaging the tires,
wear and tear, or the cost of a girl's bike in 1981.
You name your Cabbage Patch Doll Dillon, and
your stuffed koala bear Fuzzy Wuzzy. You feed

them milk and cheese, even cut a hole in Fuzzy's gray
mouth so the milk can dribble down his koala chin.
These are your children because one day, of course
you will be a mother. You are 7—you know you will.

Going Through With It

By all accounts, Tiffany Hall and Jimella Tunstall were like sisters,
    . . .Hall, 24 years old . . .was accused…of killing the pregnant
    Tunstall, 23, and the fetus that authorities say was cut from her
    womb. *Associated Press* 9/25/06
Hall "had been thinking about taking the baby for some time" from
    Tunstall, *Associated Press* 4/11/07

And the scissors are in your hands.
Feel the baby kick, rumble in greeting.
Try to guess his position. Metal pierces
skin, ruptures flesh, fat, the muscular
uterine wall. Once the baby is free
cut the cord and like the movies, wipe off
blood, bend down, suck mucus out of the
tiny nostrils. Pretend not to see the empty
husk of her belly, the blood, the blood
staining the carpet. Whatever else your hands
do, they do. All you envision is buying the baby seat,
cruising the baby aisle at Giant Eagle—
where there's formula to pick from, bottles to clean.

bough breaks

Amazing what
the brain can
            & cannot do
It cannot
make a baby
or uterus
hold tight

it cannot
make a uterus
keep its liquid secrets

what drops and slips
thru the cervix
down the canal
out the portal
to rust
            in the world
is not blood
but broken
bits of mucus, egg,
tissue, all promises
your body
never intended
to keep

Hunger

Unlucky 16 year-old bodies in trendy baby t-shirts
two sizes too small, nonchalant bellies protruding.
Lucky 21 year-old bodies that bounce back
to a size 6 after delivery. Their recklessness,

how it mocks your wedding band, framed diplomas.
Laughs at your planning, your suburban home, in it
only the dog to step over, only the husband to let
sleep. In East St. Louis a woman carved a child

from the belly of a childhood friend. Another slit
the throat of a new mother, the betrayal of her
own stillbirth still fresh. Like you, she knew the baby
hunger. How it swells, devouring the insides of strollers,

fattened bodies in cotton cuddly onesies, like you, these
women know the pang when friend after friend joyously
announces while you buy more pads. But this hunger is everything
you are told you can be, so you try to fill it, and you try and you try.

Slip Skin Study: Broken

How many licks before you get to the center of a Tootsie Pop?
The wise owl asks. If he were a reproductive endocrinologist
he would know 35 is the magic number. After that it's advanced
maternal age after that I have outlived my usefulness Bachelor's,
Master's, Ph.D, MD, CEO, CFO, tampons flushed down the toilet,
sanitary napkins too flooded to use. Here's what I can offer you now:
a silent tongue, a hushed hip, an empty lap and hands cradling
Broken egg after egg after egg. After 35 I am beyond
my expiration date. Use with caution.

At 5 weeks

Like a splinter the bleeding didn't last long.
A day, two, at the most when the pain pricked
then pricked again, business-like, curt. A miscarriage

leaves no genetic calling card like a live birth.
No grooves where the pelvic bone popped apart.
No finger-painting the marrow to say someone was here.

Memory sharpens the pain, splintering its lightning
through the body. The body, its grieving heart, its hunger,
its questioning: can we, too, not have joy last past a season?

There was no warning this muscular embrace would break.
No warning the bough would fall, the blood would flee
in mutiny, spreading down the thighs, forsaking. I have found

if I turn my head this way and see that perfect tendril of February
sun, the memory of pain comes back. If I listen to the singer's tenor,
breaking sorrow's back, the straining violin too full of beauty

to sustain, I return to the moment when I was briefly the vessel.
And then I am the vessel again slowly emptying myself of you.

The Return of the Prodigal Mother

Here's what I am supposed to want:
a husband, children, a pretty jeweled
leash. That I run thru his hands

like eel innards—you hate me for it.
That I whelped his rats, milked them even,
and that's not all I need—you hate me for that too.

Know this—I crave the wind, its lashing
promise. At night I dance untethered under
swollen clouds, let the humid air suckle my skin.

But for now, I shout through pursed and painted lips.
I kick back with a dainty-slippered foot. I breech this birth.
This time blonde, next brunette, I will come back. Again and again
      and again.

Induced

For Zoë

After the Pitocin
After the Magnesium Sulfate
After the contractions
After the migraine
After 6 centimeters
After the nurse came
After my mother came
After the vomiting
After 9 centimeters
After 10
After he whispered *push*
After the warming lamp was clicked on
After *almost there* the fourth time
After *almost there* the sixth time
I closed my eyes and the only voice I heard was my own
In the darkness a notch shifted and after me—came you

Letdown

The books say that milk letdown
feels like pins and needles
but when you're pumping at work
it's more like lungs constricting
under the crush of chlorinated water.
You know, god willing, when she's 16 or 25
you'll never be this essential again.
So remember this smothering need now,
the engorged breasts, the suction, the release.
Know the ache swelling and flowing from you,
is caused by your hands cradling plastic bottles,
that your warm, twisting baby is elsewhere,
away from you. Know the sadness will threaten
to sweep you under, each time you take out the pump
and you can't swim away from it. You must do this for her.
You must stay, you must drown.

Family Bed

Her first tumult, roundhouse, flip
little spark of flutter, little slip
when the universe tumbled through me
I plodded, heavy with importance, our
path forward. Now she curls to me
the little c to the S curve of my breast,
my nipple a breath away from her
needy lips. You say we must break her
of sleeping with mommy—with daddy.
You say two nights of no rest, of offering myself
is two nights too many—but she beckons
and when have I not heeded her call?
This love radiates, burns brighter with each
diminished night. I cannot relinquish her need.
How tiring and lovely it is to fill.

All the King's Horses

It's 5 in the morning and already I fail. Shortly
the raspy cry will start from the crib,

the thought stiffens my nipple, milk pooling
in preparation. How many times have I glared

down the clock's blue electronic glow,
don't I know, it's always too early?

Still the alarm beeps, ambitious to the second.
The minutes flee leading me straight into the brick

of this day. Awake. I should be shaking
the covers loose, my mind snapping, attacking

crucial details: shower, feed the baby, snatch bites of breakfast,
leave on time. Instead my mind slouches, grasping at dreams,

choking them, hoping they will spill the secret
of how I'm supposed to get through this day.

Thick of It

The cough is wet, the mucus clogged,
unambitious in her nine month-old throat,
still present enough to nettle, nudge her

away from sleep. My new mother ear hears
this and more—the humidifier's odd hiccup
the heat clicking, lumbering on. My husband

snores. Tomorrow waits, patiently ticking away
the night's minutes. I will bear no dreams tonight
even though they taunt and tease, whispering

their magic. In the morning we will pass an old
woman sitting alone on a bench under a tree in
autumn's last throes, gold and glorious. We will

wonder at her lack—no newspaper, no book, no
husband, to pass the time and the time, how it oozes
around her. We catch its intoxicating whiff

while rushing to work. Late again. His mood is dark,
darker still is mine, lurking, sifting the laundry list
of what's unrealized, what's left to do, but the baby

will smile then, both dimples and I will forget to remember again
this is the thick of it. He will pause at the stop sign, then we'll lurch
forward, in a futile attempt to get ahead of the morning traffic.

Two Glasses of Milk

If I were to leave them
two glasses of milk,
don't write about that,
write about the napkin
the perfect triangle tucked
around the circle of glass,
the absorbed condensation.

If I were to leave them
two glasses of milk, it would be
the tension of motherhood
and career, poet and wife
pulling like teeth at my
extended nipples until I was
greedily consumed in silence.

If I were to leave them
two glasses of milk,
even across my tombstone
would be the words:
daughter, wife, mother.
Identities like anchors,
so heavy I would carry
them even after death.

Lament for Things Found Under a Child's Bed:

Broken crayon, here you are. Once a star
now dust gives your only applause. Puzzle piece—
debris without your brethren in the frame.
One fuzzy monster slipper, never
caught on, five year-old feet fleet in their dismissal.
All things under the bedframe know love is sight
till unseen. Unseen: the haven for all lost things.

Notes

"Fade to Black" is after the article "'12 Years A Slave,' 'Mother of George,' and the aesthetic politics of filming black skin" by Ann Hornaday, *The Washington Post* 10/17/13.

"Scar Tissue" uses the Bop form created by Afaa Michael Weaver. The poem references the song title "I Know I'll Never Love This Way Again" as sung by Dionne Warwick, composed by Richard Kerr and written by Will Jennings.

"Dear Diary" is inspired by two separate events reported in the *Cleveland Plain Dealer* February of 1998, and May of 2001. The February story covered the death of 11 month-old LaShae Davis, (who died of multiple internal injuries and broken bones caused by blows to his head, chest, and abdomen). His 14 year-old father was charged with the murder. The May story covered the death of 8 week-old Diamond Miller, who was beaten to death. Her 13 year-old father was charged with her murder.

In the poem "Nights at Maya's" mzungu is Swahili for stranger, foreigner, often a white person.

"Perspective" is after a visit to Lake Nakura Regional Park in Kenya in 1997.

"One Night Stand" uses the Golden Shovel form created by Terrance Hayes. Each line ends with a word from a selected line from "The Sundays of Satin-Legs Smith" by Gwendolyn Brooks.

"Morning when a dream lingers" is after "The Dumbing Down of Love" by the group Frou Frou.

"Haint" is after an article on CNN.com.

The poem "the blond on his arm" is after a *US Weekly* article about the actor Adrien Brody and his girlfriend at the time.

"Odalisque" is after *Untitled* (Boudoir scene of nude white woman and her naked black maid, 1850's) by Félix-Jacques Moulin.

"She talks to Michael Fassbender" has an epigraph from Charles Baudelaire's poem "La Vénus Noire" believed to be to his mulatto mistress.

"At 5 weeks" is after the song "Seasons" by the artist formerly known as Terence Trent D'Arby.

"Slip Skin Study: Broken" and "The Return of the Prodigal Mother" are both after paintings of the same name by the artist Dawn Black.

"Induced" mentions two drugs commonly used in labor induction: Pitocin and magnesium sulfate, a drug used to alternately stop labor or to prevent seizures in pregnant patients with high blood pressure.

The poem "Two Glasses of Milk" references Sylvia Plath's suicide. On February 11, 1963, Plath placing her head in a gas oven. She left bread and milk for her two children, sleeping upstairs.

Biography:

Teri Ellen Cross Davis is a Cave Canem fellow and has attended the Soul Mountain Writer's Retreat, the Virginia Center for Creative Arts, and the Fine Arts Work Center in Provincetown. Her work has been published in many anthologies including, *Bum Rush The Page: A Def Poetry Jam*, *Gathering Ground: A Reader Celebrating Cave Canem's First Decade*, *Growing Up Girl*, *Full Moon on K Street: Poems About Washington, DC*, and *Check the Rhyme: An Anthology of Female Poets & Emcees*. Her work can also be read in the following publications: *Beltway Poetry Quarterly*, *Gargoyle*, *Natural Bridge*, *The Sligo Journal*, *ArLiJo*, *Mi Poesias*, *Torch*, *Poet Lore*, *North American Review* and the *Puerto Del Sol* blog. She currently lives in Silver Spring, Maryland with her husband, poet Hayes Davis and their two children.

Photo by Mig Dooley Photography

Poetry from Gival Press

12: Sonnets for the Zodiac by John Gosslee

Adama: Poème / Adama: Poem by Céline Zins with English translation by Peter Schulman

Bones Washed in Wine: Flint Shards from Sussex and *Bliss* by Jeff Mann

Box of Blue Horses by Lisa Graley

Camciones para una sola cuerda / Songs for a Single String by Jesús Gardea with English translation by Robert L. Giron

Dervish by Gerard Wozek

The Great Canopy by Paula Goldman

Grip by Yvette Neisser Moreno

Haint by Teri Ellen Cross Davis

Honey by Richard Carr

Let Orpheus Take Your Hand by George Klawitter

Metamorphosis of the Serpent God by Robert L. Giron

Museum of False Starts by Chip Livingston

On the Altar of Greece by Donna J. Gelagotis Lee

On the Tongue by Jeff Mann

The Nature Sonnets by Jill Williams

The Origin of the Milky Way by Barbara Louise Ungar

Poetic Voices Without Borders edited by Robert L. Giron

Poetic Voices Without Borders 2 edited by Robert L. Giron

Prosody in England and Elsewhere: A Comparative Approach by Leonardo Malcovati

Protection by Gregg Shapiro

Psaltery and Serpentines by Cecilia Martínez-Gil

Refugee by Vladimir Levchev

The Silent Art by Clifford Bernier

Some Wonder by Eric Nelson

Songs for the Spirit by Robert L. Giron
Sweet to Burn by Beverly Burch
Tickets for a Closing Play by Janet I. Buck
Voyeur by Rich Murphy
We Deserve the Gods We Ask For by Seth Brady Tucker
Where a Poet Ought Not / Où c'qui faut pas by G. Tod Slone

For a complete list of Gival Press titles, visit: *www.givalpress.com*.

Books available from Follett, Ingram, your favorite bookstore, on-line booksellers, or directly from Gival Press.

Gival Press, LLC
PO Box 3812
Arlington, VA 22203
givalpress@yahoo.com
703.351.0079